TOUCHSTONE

By
Nancy M Bell

©2015

Touchstone
Copyright © 2015 Nancy M Bell

All rights reserved. No part of this book may be reproduced in any form or by any electronic or mechanical means including information storage and retrieval systems without written permission from the author, except by a reviewer, who may quote brief passages in a review

First Edition

ISBN-13: 978-1519517500
ISBN-10: 1519517505

Cover Photo Copyright 2015 Nancy M Bell

Published by Nancy M Bell

Printed in the United States of America

Touchstone

We are linked by love
You and I
You have been my steadfast friend
My anchor in the stormy seas
My safe rock on which to stand
And survey my uncertainties

The sharer of my secrets
The keeper of the wings of my spirit
You have given so much
And asked so little
Touchstone of my soul
Transcending even the distance of death.

Tide

Squatting on the rocks in the bay
I watch the tide come in
Little trickle by little trickle
Filling the tiny spaces between the pebbles
Floating the crabs from their niches

Each tiny wave a part of the whole
Innocuously slipping their way toward the cedars
Clear crystal emerald covering the shingle
Sighing the eternal song
Echoed in the womb

The tide is coming in
Sliding up the shore
Sure and steady as mothers love.

Spring

Once on the meadow
Down by the stream
Little people talking
Little people singing

Trees and bulrush growing
Grass and flowers swaying
Life and love unfolding
Time and wars forgotten

Raindrops falling
Sunshine smiling
Dewdrops shining
SPRING

Musing on a June Afternoon

On this blue and green day in June
The swallows dive above the daisies
The butterflies play below
A soft breeze cuddles the lilacs
And tousles the Manitoba maples

June is such a busy month
The month for haying
But also the month to lie in the dew wet grass
And breathe the crystalline star music of the night

The greens of June, so bright and new
The sun; June brilliant
The grackles chase across the sheep meadow in a cloud
And the finches sing in the crabapple by the door
A narrow waisted wasp crawls on the window sill
And a hawk floats on the wind over the triticale field

Autumn Foreshadow

There is an autumn slant to the sun
The wind has the breath of October to it
Though the maples show no glimmer of gold

Overhead the gulls wheel against the blue and pewter
of the sky
Now and then a breast flashing silver
The August dry corn gossips with the wind
And tosses its heads of silk
Beside the rows of downed barley

Black birds flock and line the wires
Then lift together with a ripple of wings in the wind
And dance in a black cloud over the golden straw
Riding the wind as one entity

It is only August
But autumn whispers in the air.

Silence That is Full of Sound

Silence that is filled with sound
For those with hearts to hear
Early dawn light in the mists of morning bound
The water breathes upon the shore, so clear

Frog music trills and the call of the loon echoes through the pale light
The Great Blue Heron makes his ungainly, graceful, silent flight
His wings sweeping through the tendrils of mist in delight

Somewhere a fish takes to the air and falls back into the brackish
Water with a gentle splash
There is a glorious cacophony of wild goose music as they appear
From out of the mist and quickly disappear
Leaving the sound of the strength of their wings in wind
Sounds that illuminate the inner silences of the heart and there are twinned.

Rain

The rain will always be
Always the same
And eons from now in this very spot
The rain will still fall
And the wind's music ring
But I will no longer be; anywhere
But then no one will care
If I laughed or cried while the rain fell
They will only know
That the rain still falls.

Silent World

Let me be a part of you
O Silent World
Where others hear only silence
Let me hear the wind talking
Let me see the smile of sun on alfalfa bloom
Take the pungent perfume of the earth into my lungs

Let me draw peace
From the evening light on the fields
And the gossip of the trees
Give me the kinship of the spirits
Of earth and sky
Of fire and water
Of the deep well of silence that abides at the center
O let me a part of you Silent World
You, who are everything and nothing.

Dancing in the Moon

The moonlight is strong through my window
The spring equinox draws near
On the beams that slant across the sill
My ancient lover comes riding

The tiny part of me who remembers still
Rises to dance in the moonlight
Entwining and joining
Shining like motes of brighter light
Against the silver of the moon

Memories flood through me, wild and strong
I am coming home, again and again
In a wild whirl of remembrance
I know I must remember the words
I speak them into the mouth of my other self

When the sun falls bright across my bed
I search for the words
But they have no place in this time
I can almost remember them though
And the steps of the dance in the moonlight

Broken Dreams

Gently, I behold this delicate crystal thing
That we have named Love
Watching as it swings in the wind
And sparkles in the sun
So beautiful and fragile
It hurts to watch it die

Bits at a time little pieces break off
They fall and are silvered on the floor
Together the pieces used to be something
But this crystal dust on the floor is nothing

Moving like figures in an old mirror
I see the images dance by and around me
They don't belong to me anymore
Here and there the mirror is blemished
Where someone glued a broken piece back in place
All that is left is the glue

Watching the beauty fade and become mist in my fingers
I surrender to the loneliness, anger and fear that are left.

Nostalgia

Bittersweet; nibbling at the toes of my subconscious
Memories of long past summer days
Evoked by the essence of green cut hay
A myriad of days
Wrapped up in the rustle of ripening wheat

Shimmering moonlight
Freeing the ghosts locked away in memory
Sending them shouting and galloping once again
Through the now silent dark
Plunging me back into half-forgotten dreams
And half-remembered loves

Sweet moon shadowed innocence of youth.

Time for Forever

If you and I had the time
We could make something of this
But we are like two snowflakes
Caught in a blizzard
Grasping hands as life whirls us by one another

And so we must go
But for a time
We can forget that there was a yesterday
Or there is a tomorrow
So when the time comes to say farewell
We can smile
Because we always knew
We never had the time for forever.

Charms

I ain't got no pretty face
And all my charms are in the bracelet on my wrist
I can't even offer you money or power
And important friends

All I can give you is all that I am
A shoulder to lean on
And peace without lies

Even though you're hear today
And tomorrow gone

All I have worth giving is me.

I Shall Go On Dreaming

I shall go on dreaming
For the things that might have been
Remembering my yesterdays
When all the world was mine

The times and the hours
When we laughed and played and sang
We always knew that it would end
I just didn't understand

I wanted to believe our love
Was like the sun, eternal
I wanted to believe our fun
Would never have to end
We wished that summer would always be
Golden sun and cool soft moon

We always knew that it would end
I just wanted to believe.

Yesterday's Last Day

This is the last day of yesterday
It can be no other way
Every other day will be tomorrow
Where joy will not be borrowed

I am closing the door on sadness
Offering myself forgiveness
No more misty dreaming of the past
I'm seeking a promise that will last

No walking with memory's guidebook in hand
Revisiting places we played on the strand
With somehow tomorrow drifting away
Until I'm caught forever in the last day of yesterday

So now I'm searching through the clouds for tomorrow
Ignoring the beaconing sighs of yesterday's sorrow
I'm leaving behind this lonely madness
And closing the door on sadness.

Who Are You?

Who are you that you can touch me so?
Touch my heart with your eyes?
Hold me with your smile

Who are you that you draw me into your soul?
Making me oblivious to everything
Except that we are together in the same universe
We are the universe

Who are you?
But I know
Somehow from the first I've known
Somewhere, in sometime
We have known one another
We have been one

Even now, separated by other lives
I can't deny the voice in my heart
Or the light through your eyes

Afterglow

How long can I stay steeping
In this afterglow of love
Watching as it shimmers
In the effervescent light

Like dreams gone sleeping
On the pearl gray breast of doves
Distant lights that glimmer
Through the blackness of the night

Not near enough to touch again
But close enough to cause pain.

Wisdom

Wisdom is written in the star fire
Secrets in the silver of the dark sea
Ancient words that I thought I would no longer require
Rhythms that still rule in me

Listen to the wisdom speak
Let it echo in your heart
Find the courage not to break
In wisdom there is no gentle part.

Wind Dance

The winds have sent the sun
To silver the dance of the sea
Blowing the tide to the shingle
Striking silver fire from the spindrift spangle
Chasing the sunset through clouds clothed in pewter
Then like a benevolent benefactor
The light pulls treasure from where none should be
Throwing argent coin into the sea
Liquid silver sliding up the glistening rocks
Melting into the darkness under the docks.

Taboo

Through this dark and ancient place I go
You can hear the sea
You can remember the sun
But they are not present here

There are spirits here though
I can feel them around me
They touch me but only to shun
To push me from here

Climbing through the cedars time seems to slow
I emerge on the cliff above the trees
The old magic stays in the hollow while I stand in the sun
The wind and sun burn away the fear.

IF

If I told you I was lonely
Would you come to me?

If I told you I was sad
Would you cry with me?

If I told you I felt broken
Would you mend me?

If I told you that my stars were gone
Would you light them with the candles in your heart?

If I told you I was happy
Would you rejoice with me?

If I told you it was raining
Would you walk with me?

If I told you I loved you
Would you love me?

Fire

Those few moments between sleep and waking
Watching you chest rise and fall in your sleeping
Nestled together in the peace of love and trust

After you have gone as I know you must
These are the moments that will haunt my dreams with desire
When you no longer care to kindle me with your fire.

Snowflake

Born in the bosom of the cloud the crystal snowflake drifts
Lighting softly on the tip of the mountain
Capturing the shine of the moon as a gift
Throwing the light back in a tiny shimmering fountain
A burst of coruscating colour, glistening in the distance
Marks the beautiful, brief magic existence.

Miracle

I have watched it every year
Yet each time I cannot
Help but wonder
At the miracle of Spring.

Gone

When I stop at times
And realize just how happy I am
I'm afraid of when it will end.

I hide fear and sometimes wish
That we had never been this happy
I grow cold and still inside
Because I know that someday he will leave

Our lives are so short
Eons from now the wind will still walk this beach
But our footprints will not be there to erase
The cold still knowledge lingers in my heart
Telling me that not even gentle sunlight will melt it
after he is gone.

Memories from a Honeymoon
May 1977

I remember green English fields and coal fires
Rain and Jubilee banners
Pigeons in Trafalgar Square
Walking through Hyde Park in the sun
Feeling the presence of ghosts from the past

And then Paris, City of flowers and bridges
Notre Dame rising from the stones
As if it has always been there
Inside the candles shining in the dark

I remember a pink rosebush in a park
Near the Eiffel Tower and more pigeons
Walking on the Champs Elysie in the rain
Sitting a little café with a café au lait
That cost a buck a cup
Crepes with strawberry jam from a street vendor

Zurich's mountains and lake
A white swan in the river at dawn
And a hotel that was closed
Red roofs and cobble streets
Alpine flowers on the slopes and sweet mountain air

Amsterdam, city of canals
Dam Square and more pigeons
The Red Light District and a hungry alley cat
Walking along the Prinsengrache and Damrack
McDonald's at last
Shopping the bustling streets
Wheels of cheese and fish markets
French fries with mayonnaise, and more rain
And over it all everlasting love.

Carpets and Mirrors

Every once in a while
Some soft talking man comes along
Speaking gently and sweet
Like mountains at sunrise

And he takes me for a ride
On his magic carpet made of dreams
But it always seems that the carpet unravels
And the dreams all disappear

Leaving me holding only a handful of memories
And a vague reflection in the mirror
Of mountains in the rain.

Daddy

I was just a little girl
When Daddy went away
I couldn't understand it then
I don't understand it now

"Cause he's been gone
For oh so long
And Mommy looks so sad
Since Daddy's gone away

He used to read me picture books at night
He built me a doll house
But now it needs repairs

My Mommy tries to act the same
But I know something's wrong
Even though I'm just a little girl
Cause Daddy's gone to war.

Summer Memories

Old memories stir and my heart aches to renew them
The chill edge to the night air
The stillness hanging heavy with frog music
For the moonlight turning the still lake to ice
For the taste of the wind and banners
Of the birch trees in the marsh flung
against the burning of the dying day
To see again the brilliance of sun on blue water
And the fir trees splashed against the sky
Listen again to the whisper of the trees
And the cry of the loons through the mist a dawn.

The Searcher

Weary world wanderer
Returned to home at last
Sheltered and protected
By the place that loves you best

Peace in singing fir trees
Refreshed by sea spun spray
Gentle giants grace your shore
Protected, just as you

Morning sun burns off the mist
Revealing harbors safe
After years of endless searching
Your heart has found its home.

Touchstone

We are linked by love
You and I
You have been my steadfast friend
My anchor in the stormy seas
My safe rock on which to stand
And survey my uncertainties

The sharer of my secrets
The keeper of the wings of my spirit
You have given so much
And asked so little
Touchstone of my soul
Transcending even the distance of death.

My Door

Do you suppose he could have forgotten
the way to my door?
I think he must, for he isn't there
I have waited and waited
But I can't wait no more
I love him
But love's endurance grows bare
And I know he has forgotten
The way to my door.

Silent Horses

Do you often wonder why love is the way it is
How it happens so easily
Stealing softly through the night
Catching you unaware
Wriggling under you skin

Riding silent horses in the moonlight
Never leaving as quietly
Nor as painlessly as it came.

Still in Love

I am still in love
Not with you anymore
But with your memory
The memory of what we had
And what we were to each other

I am in love still
With the happiness we shared
And the smiles we gave each other
With the summer days we lived together
And the love we shared.

Bartholomew Kitten

Little of bundle of life that you were
Held now in my hands
Stroking you soft head gently
Though now it no longer matters

Remembering all the times in our brief acquaintance
That you made me smile
And now I cry
All I can do is lay you in grass and soft earth

And hold you forever in my heart.

Never

Youth is over, seemingly in a glance
Sun filled memories crowd the corners of my heart
Misty yesterdays dance
Half remembered dreams set apart
The years join hands
The ache inside me expands
Because we will never share these days again.

Ingredients for Happiness

Trees and soft sunshine
Flowers and wild creatures
Wind in the poplar trees like bells
Rivers curling through green valleys
But also soft summer rain
And autumn trees
Green grass turned to russet
Pine shavings in my horse's stall
And sunlight on your face.

Adversity

If there had been no such yesterday
This sorrow would not now be staining my heart
I could still smile at the morning sun breaking the day
Without quietly remembering that once you were there
to be a part

I have learned at the cost of my innocence
That love and happiness may not stay on the same side
of the fence
And that life can become an ache that binds
A cruel charade of some kind

But bitterness burns off like mist on the river
Given enough time
Leaving me holding only the hurt
Cupped in the bleeding hollow of my heart
I embrace the knowledge, that one morning
When the sun warms the frosty rust kissed river grass
My life once again will flow irrevocably forward.

Christmas Magic

Where is that Christmas feeling I had as a child?
The wide eyed wonderment
The thrill of soft snow on my cheeks
What happened to the girl who felt tears
Start in her throat when she sang carols by the tree?

But somewhere in my wanderings tonight…
Perhaps in the music of the wind through the snow
laden boughs
Or in the dance of the white flakes coming down
In the silence of the night and the trees
I found her again in the moonlit snow

Stirring awake inside me to stand with head thrown
back
To watch the stars and gaze in silent rapture
At the snow encrusted woods
The child inside survives the slip of years.

Last Leaf

The last leaf has been peeled
From the last tree in the lane
Slapped to the field
By November's bleak rain

Black the bark glistens in the fading night
Frosty tears melting as the watery dawn is born
Bare are the branches stretched forth to the light
Trying vainly to hold the pink, grey silver morn

Piercing the heart
Catching the breath
Sorrowing wildly for summer's depart
Winter coming fleetly to freeze the heart.

Crystal Stair

This love that I don't speak with my tongue
I speak with my hands and when my songs are sung
I speak with my eyes and with my thoughts too

With my heart I can touch you
And know that you have heard
Even though my mouth oft times speaks other words

You spirit and mine
Meet above us and entwine
Grow the wings of hawks
Waltz where the east wind walks
Climb the crystal stair
Leaving only their sharp hawk cry lingering in the air.

Chestnut Candles

The chestnut candles are lit with the white blooms
That gleam in the misty gloom
Rain drips like wax from the fingered leaves
Falling onto the restless mat that the grasses weave

Somewhere nearby the lilacs are in flower
The heady fragrance sweet in the rain shower
Mingling with the damp earth smell of newly plowed terrain
Joy is ignited in my heart by the chestnut candles in the rain.

Seagulls and Shining Water

Looking back, I can see where some of my life
Has ridden by in dark strife
But there have been times when the seagulls have flown
Above the shining water and laughed as they were windblown
And I remember them most

But the dark birds are there and they return to haunt
And their memories taunt
Though they showed me wisdom when I was lost
More than the seagulls and shining water, but at a cost.

Love me To-night

Love me to-night
Tomorrow may never become reality
But to-night:
Your breath on my skin
This is all the reality I need

When the daylight comes
No one will ever know that our hearts leaped as one
We will walk our separate paths
Forget that our souls entwined
Deny the truth:
That for a moment we lived.

Ancient Touch

As I leave the path of ferns near the carved pole
And enter this once dark place
A breeze from the sea caresses my face
I feel a welcome that touches my soul
It lifts my head and fills my sight with gold and jade
It seems the sun shines
Although the clearing is full of forest shade

I am strong, I am free
For just a moment, I am not just me
But a lithe limbed warrior, a hunter
I breathe the magic of the encounter

The spirits have touched me and it is warm.

Wait

If I could keep the world from turning
Just for a while
Give me some time to catch up with myself

But the world keeps on turning
Time keeps on whirling
And I just keep falling so much farther behind.

Please

Do you remember the days when we smiled?
Do you remember the days when we laughed?
The days we were free in the sun and the wind
The days when we loved
Do you remember?
Please.

Secretariat

You were bred to win
And born to race
While still a colt you left
Your rolling Meadow fields
Forever

Destined to show that dreams
Can still come true
The essence of power and beauty
Running for love of it
Running for yourself
Honestly and truly

The sun was your spotlight
You were the ruler
The world your minions
Like your daddy's name a Bold Ruler
And like your momma's truly Something Royal

And now each time we see a flaming chestnut
The world looks again hoping that it's you
Knowing that it never will be again.

May Moonlight

Deep in the dark of the woodland valley
The moonlight sifts through the trees
Weaving dappled patterns over the silver sand

High on the hill in the moonlight
We sit and watch the night
Here and there like angel down
The May white apples bloom

The stars above in the velvet sky
Are pale and wan tonight
In awe of the shimmering moon
All nature's in tune with our love.

Winter Morning

Snow silvered branches spread against the pearl velvet
of the sky
Bare trunks a dark slash against the white-blue snow
The frosty filigreed branches glow with illumination
The pale light gathered and thrown upwards by the
fields they guard
The Goddess is holding her breath
There is no colour on this palette
Only shades of silver pewter
The pale blue-white of snow and shadow
And the stark black wounds of the trees
Stitching the earth to the sky.

Solstice

A whisper of white
in the wintry wood
Silver sifting softly
Shimmering snow shifting
Moonlight magnifying the memory
of trees in the shadows
The bitter breath of the frigid frost
borne on the cutting crystal breeze
Moon woken diamonds glitter
In the riddling rhyme of
Branches stretched against the pearl black night
Teetering on the tip of beauty
The Winter Solstice slides down this long night
To embrace the light.

Seduced by the Storm

There is something sweetly seductive
About a wild winter storm
A restlessness that urges me out
Into the frenzy of storm demons howling down the sky

The dance of energy exchange
Charging the air as it races
From high pressure to low
Heavy arctic air challenging and mating
With the moisture laden sweet southern jet stream

Their passion manifested in myriad snowflakes
Thrown with heady abandon
Down the winds of their union.

Seasons

Love is only a season in our lives

Spring like, Blowing hot
Contrarily tied with winter's knot

Summer; love's reflection
meadows full of clover drift
Passing swift

Autumn light
Stark and bright
Bees fleeing winter seek their hives

Winter; sharp and brittle
Makes Love's light too little
Lost, with no direction

Love may be only a season
But our lives are ruled by seasons.

The Fog

I wandered with him
Through the fog
Only the two of us
Lost in the fog

The horse's shoulders butted forward
Cutting through the fog
Carrying me safely toward home
Through the fog

His neck arched before me
Stronger than the fog
His hooves surely treading
Through the fog

Since the beginning he has carried me
Lost in the fog
At the last he will safely take me
Through the fog.

Cortes

This island;
Speaks to me of hearts flung high
And courage pinned against the sky
Shows me a love with roots that stand
As deep and steadfast as this land
The granite rises where eagles cry
The sea waves wash it with their sigh
On cliff tops crowning fir trees stand

They guard against the coming storm
Though change is coming every where
The island remains what it will be

A refuge from the rising swarm
What a simple friendship they share
The Island and the sea.

Afraid

Afraid to be with you
And afraid to be alone
Torn between the trembling uncertainties
And the securities of my isolation
My mind in restless circles wheeling
Answer all my questions with more.

Compromise

What more can I say
That hasn't been said
What more can I do
That hasn't been done

I cannot crawl;
I will not beg
Halfway is all
that my battered pride will allow

If you had only stretched out a hand
Turned your head in my direction
Let the sunlight of your smile
Warm for a little while.

Summer's End

Now the summer is gone in a glance
Sun warm memories crowd the corners of my heart
Misty yesterdays dance
With half remembered dreams; empty arms held apart

The years join hands
And the ache inside expands
Because we can never share these days again.

Lost in the Choices

Dreams that are more than my realities
Hold me captive from myself
Or is it my realities
Holding me captive from my dreams?

Awash in confusion
My spirit twisted in agitation
I am no longer sure what is me
Who do I want to be?

Shall I stay safe and secure
With the dawn breeze of my lover's breath in my hair
Or strong and alone with the wind of autumn
Stroking its fingers against my face

Choices that seem right;
Choices that seem wrong;
I am lost in the choices.

Song to my Leaving

Do not leave us
Do not leave us
Ferns grasp at my wrist

Stay with us
Stay with us
Salal rustles at my knees

Here with us
Here with us
The Laurel whispers sweet and sure

Linger here
Linger here
The tide creeps up the shore

Love me
Love me
The wind tugs at my hand

Echoed by the sun, the plaintive cry of gulls
Mirrors the pain in my heart
As I answer what I must

I cannot stay
I cannot stay.